Beetle

Iulid

Banana slug

Cicada

Earthworm

Fly

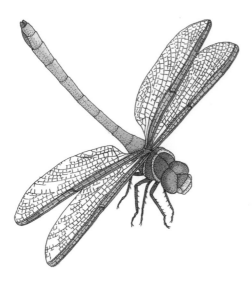

Published by
Princeton Architectural Press
202 Warren Street
Hudson, New York 12534
www.papress.com

Originally published in French as *Le Livre Aux Petites Bêtes*
© Editions Belin / Humensis, 2018

Translated from the French by Yolanda Stern Broad

ISBN 978-1-61689-974-5
Library of Congress Control Number: 2020938787

Nathalie Tordjman

THE BOOK OF TINY CREATURES

Illustrated by

Julien Norwood & Emmanuelle Tchoukriel

Princeton Architectural Press · New York

Contents

WHO ARE THE TINY CREATURES? 08

Such diversity! 10

Under a magnifying glass » Tiny creatures with soft bodies

Reproduction 12

Quiz » Four ways to lay eggs

Growing 14

Under a magnifying glass » All kinds of ways to grow

Big zoom » Where do tiny creatures go in winter?

My observatory » On the balcony

LIFE IN THE SKY 20

Flying 22

Under a magnifying glass » Who uses four wings to fly?

Meals on the fly 24

Little workshop » Catch a tiny creature!

In case of attack 26

Under a magnifying glass » Midair hunting

Big zoom » Pollinators at work

My observatory » In the meadow

CLOSE TO THE GROUND 32

Walking, crawling 34
Little workshop » Build a snail terrarium!

What feasts! 36
Under a magnifying glass » Meals for large animals

Cunning and combat 38
Little workshop » Set up shelters in your garden!
Big zoom » Ant society
My observatory » In the forest

IN THE WATER 44

Swimming 46
Under a magnifying glass » Above the water

Breathing in the water 48
Under a magnifying glass » How aquatic larvae breathe

Eating, cleaning 50
Quiz » Four ways to eat
Big zoom » Life in the water
My observatory » At the seashore

INCREDIBLE CREATURES 56

World records 58

The most beautiful butterflies 60

Pests 62

Nocturnal creatures 64

Guests in our homes 66

The insect orchestra 68
Answers to questions 68
Index of tiny creatures 69

WHO ARE THE TINY CREATURES?

SUCH DIVERSITY!

The bodies of tiny creatures are set up in many different ways.

Three big groups

✳ **Mollusks,** such as snails, have soft, always-moist bodies, which may be protected by a shell. Most of them only have one foot.

✳ **Annelids,** or worms, have a soft body, formed out of a series of rings, and no feet.

✳ **Arthropods** have bodies protected by a hardened layer, called a cuticle, and articulated feet. They include insects, arachnids, myriapods, and crustaceans.

Arthropods: The most numerous group

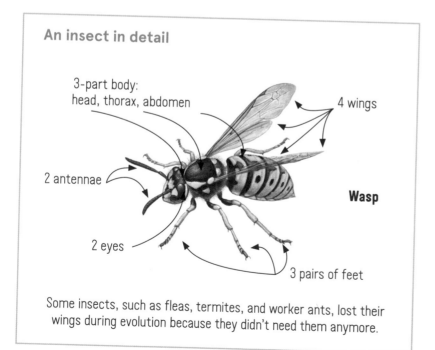

An insect in detail

3-part body: head, thorax, abdomen

4 wings

2 antennae

Wasp

2 eyes

3 pairs of feet

Some insects, such as fleas, termites, and worker ants, lost their wings during evolution because they didn't need them anymore.

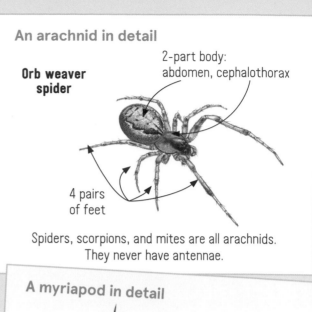

An arachnid in detail

Orb weaver spider

2-part body: abdomen, cephalothorax

4 pairs of feet

Spiders, scorpions, and mites are all arachnids. They never have antennae.

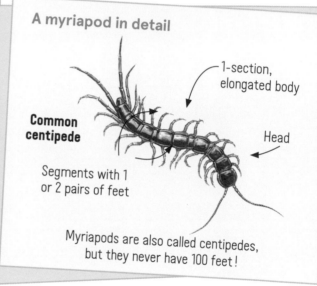

A myriapod in detail

1-section, elongated body

Common centipede

Head

Segments with 1 or 2 pairs of feet

Myriapods are also called centipedes, but they never have 100 feet!

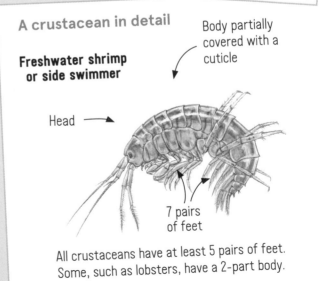

A crustacean in detail

Body partially covered with a cuticle

Freshwater shrimp or side swimmer

Head

7 pairs of feet

All crustaceans have at least 5 pairs of feet. Some, such as lobsters, have a 2-part body.

Tiny creatures with soft bodies

Mollusks

Grove snail

Garden snail

Cellar slug

Flat periwinkle

Rustic limpet

Pond snail

Annelids

Earthworm or night crawler

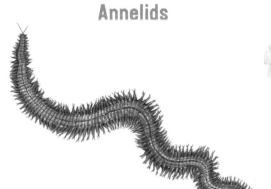

Clam worm or Nereis

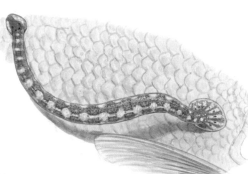

Fish bloodsucker

REPRODUCTION

There are so many tiny creatures because they have such an astounding ability to reproduce.

Male-female couples

Most arthropods pair up as a male and a female. Then the couple separates, and the female lays eggs.

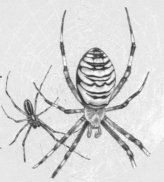

The male spider—in this case, a wasp spider—is often smaller than the female... who mustn't mistake him for prey!

Many possibilities for mating

Snails, slugs, worms, and some crustaceans are hermaphrodites (both male and female). After mating, each lays its own eggs. Some mollusks, such as flat oysters, change sex during their lives. Female aphids, for their part, give birth to their offspring without mating with a male. This is called parthenogenesis.

Operation reproduction!

To meet up, the male and female send each other messages. A female butterfly attracts a male by sending a fragrant message.

The male field cricket attracts the female by chirring, or stridulating, outside his burrow.

Where to lay eggs?

✳ The female praying mantis lays 200 to 300 eggs in air-hardening foam in egg cases called oothecae.

✳ The female garden tiger moth lays 200 to 400 eggs under the leaves of a plant.

✳ The female tarantula wolf spider weaves a silk cocoon around about 100 eggs, then carries them under her abdomen.

✳ A snail digs a hole where it lays between 50 and 100 eggs.

Four ways to lay eggs

1. **After mating, the female azure damselfly lays eggs by...**

   A releasing her eggs in flight.

   B protecting her eggs in a cocoon.

   C dipping her abdomen in water.

2. **When the female hazelnut weevil is ready to lay her eggs, she...**

   A pierces a young hazelnut.

   B catches a worm.

   C digs a hole in the ground.

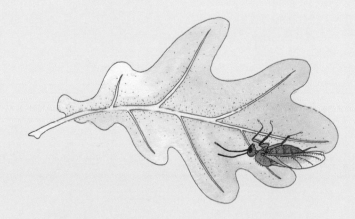

3. **The female dung beetle lays her eggs in a ball of droppings that she...**

   A sits on until they hatch.

   B hides in the ground.

   C wraps in silk.

4. **The female gall wasp lays her eggs on a leaf that...**

   A immediately withers.

   B twists up slowly.

   C produces a big growth called a gall.

GROWING

The offspring of tiny creatures are called larvae. They don't always look like their parents!

Weird-looking beasties

When they come out of their eggs, lots of larvae look very different from their parents. They don't live in the same place as their parents and don't eat the same way.

Rose chafer larvae get around by creeping on the ground; they feed on dead plants.

Adult rose chafers fly from flower to flower and graze on the petals.

Miniature adults

Some young, such as praying mantises or crickets, look the same as the adults, even if they don't yet have functional reproductive organs or wings. They feed the same way.

Resourceful young

Most often, the young manage fine without the help of their parents. The mother lays her eggs beside a cache of pollen, tender leaves, or small prey, so the larvae can feed themselves as soon as they hatch from their eggs.

Some parents watch over their young.

✳ Female parent bugs protect their young until they scatter after molting for the first time.

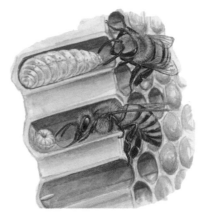

✳ Honeybee larvae have several nurses to protect and feed them.

✳ After her eggs hatch, the female wolf spider carries her young on her back for a week, holding them on with silk threads.

All kinds of ways to grow

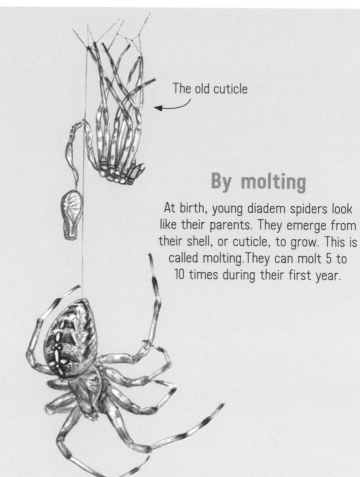

The old cuticle

By molting

At birth, young diadem spiders look like their parents. They emerge from their shell, or cuticle, to grow. This is called molting. They can molt 5 to 10 times during their first year.

Continuously

Cheese snails are born with a thin, pale shell covered with hairs and grow by coiling in a spiral. Every time they take a break from building their shell, a little striated wrinkle is formed.

Through metamorphosis

1. The seven-spot ladybug's **larvae** pierce their eggshell. They use their 6 feet and abdominal bristles (false legs located on their underside) to get around.

2. The larvae **molt** 3 times. Each time, they grow. They measure up to half an inch (12 mm) in length.

3. Once they are all plumped up, the larvae stop eating and stop moving. They have become **nymphs**. Their organs rearrange themselves, and their wings form.

4. They are **metamorphosing**. When the adults leave their cuticle, they are very pale. Their rigid wings take on color, with a number of spots that won't change again. They live one year.

Where do tiny creatures go in winter?

Tiny creatures need warmth to be active, develop, and reproduce. Winter is a difficult time. Each creature has its own method of survival.

Underground!

* In the summer, male cicadas sing to attract females. Then they lay their eggs inside twigs.

* In the fall, the adult cicadas die, and their larvae emerge from their shells. They drop to the ground and bury themselves in the soil. They remain there for 3 to 4 years. All they eat is tree-root sap.

* After the fourth summer, the larvae become nymphs. They metamorphose into adults and come out of the ground

Most adult insects die before winter arrives. During the cold season, onlythe eggs, larvae, and nymphs stay alive.

Take shelter!

* Millipedes, wood lice, some spiders, and a few insects such as earwigs or common brimstones spend the winter as adults. They take shelter, and their hemolymph (their equivalent of blood) contains an antifreeze that keeps them from freezing to death.

Julids are vegetarian millipedes. They live for several years. During the winter, they burrow into the ground or take shelter in the humid cellars of houses to keep from getting cold.

In hot countries!

1. In the fall, the painted ladies leave European gardens. They fly south, borne on the wind. Some of them journey 4,400 miles (7,000 km) to tropical Africa, where they reproduce.

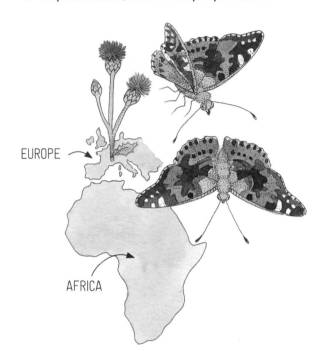

EUROPE

AFRICA

2. In the warm African climate, their life cycles are faster and therefore more numerous. When the temperatures get too hot, the last-born leave to go north.

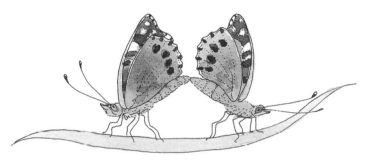

Mating

4. When summer comes, the caterpillars plump up and stop eating. They come to a standstill as nymph before metamorphosing into butterflies. Then the butterflies feed on the nectar of flowers to build up their strength. They leave for Africa in the fall.

3. In the spring, they arrive in European gardens, where they lay their eggs. Soon afterward, the caterpillars come out of their eggs.

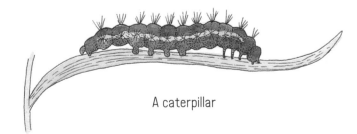

A caterpillar

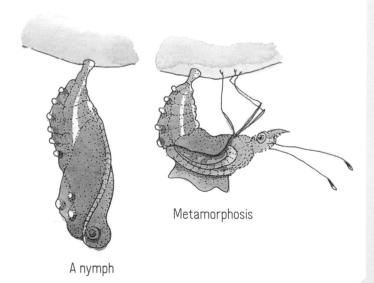

A nymph

Metamorphosis

On the balcony

Adonis blue butterfly

Ants

Aphids

Gray garden slug

Offspring of green shield bug

Ladybug larva

Garden snail

My observatory

1. What kind of larva devours aphids?

2. Who looks for moisture under a flowerpot?

3. Who bores a hole in rosebush leaves?

4. Who feasts on clover leaves?

Wood lice

18

Hoverfly

Orb weaver spiderweb

Bumblebee

Seven-spot ladybug

Adonis blue caterpillar

Green shield bug

Leaf-cutter bee

Black spruce weevil

5. Who makes lace on the edges of ivy leaves?

6. What came out of its hiding place before nightfall?

7. Who sucks on mallow leaf sap?

8. What has stuck itself to the flowerpot?

LIFE IN THE SKY

FLYING

**Among the tiny creatures,
only certain insects know how to fly.**

The wings appear

Insects have to be adults to fly. It is only after their final molt, or after metamorphosis, that their wings form. But the wings are all crumpled and can't be spread until they've absorbed air and the insect's hemolymph (its equivalent of blood) has inflated the veins on its wings.

Wings for flying

Most insects use the 2 or 4 wings attached to their thorax to fly. They flap them at high speed, mostly front to back, tilting. Their body draws what looks like a figure 8 in the air. A bee's wings vibrate 200 times per second and those of a fly as many as 500 times per second.

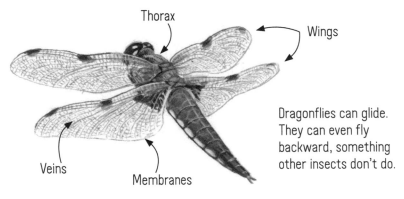

Four-spotted skimmer

Thorax

Wings

Veins

Membranes

Dragonflies can glide. They can even fly backward, something other insects don't do.

In the sky...without wings!

Tiny spiders and certain caterpillars manufacture long silk threads to get airborne on the wind. They can cover several kilometers!

Who uses two wings to fly?

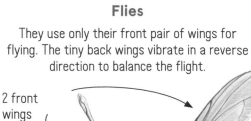

Flies

They use only their front pair of wings for flying. The tiny back wings vibrate in a reverse direction to balance the flight.

2 front wings

2 back wings

Beetles

Their 2 front wings, called elytra, protect their 2 back wings, which are used for flying.

2 thick, rigid elytra

2 large back wings

Locusts

They take off by jumping, then beat their wings or extend their leap by gliding.

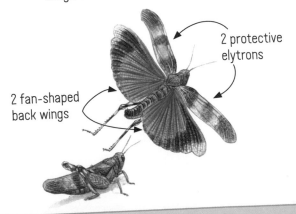

2 protective elytrons

2 fan-shaped back wings

Who uses four wings to fly?

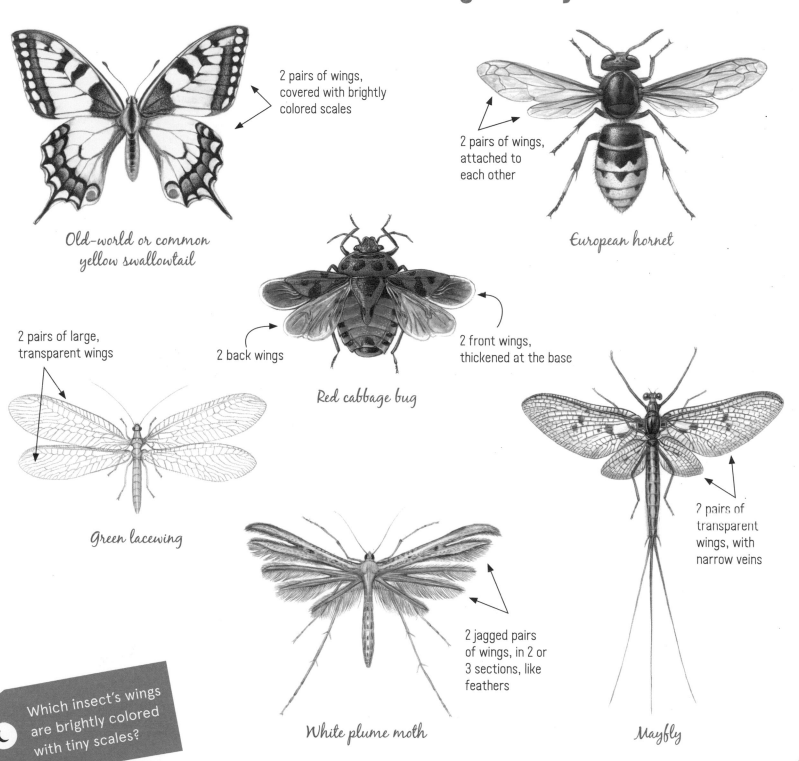

2 pairs of wings, covered with brightly colored scales

Old-world or common yellow swallowtail

2 pairs of wings, attached to each other

European hornet

2 pairs of large, transparent wings

2 back wings

2 front wings, thickened at the base

Red cabbage bug

Green lacewing

? pairs of transparent wings, with narrow veins

2 jagged pairs of wings, in 2 or 3 sections, like feathers

White plume moth

Mayfly

Which insect's wings are brightly colored with tiny scales?

MEALS ON THE FLY

Very few insects can feed themselves in flight. Most need to land to eat.

A proboscis for drinking

Many insects feed only on liquid foods. Bees lick nectar from the heart of flowers with their long tongue, while butterflies pump it with their proboscis.

The hummingbird hawk moth is one of the rare butterflies that eat while flying in place.

Mandibles for grinding

Other insects cut up their food with their mouth, which comes equipped with solid dentate patches. Some of them hunt creatures smaller than they are, or they feed on leaves or grass.

Grasshoppers cut leaves with their mandibles.

Bite, bite, bite!

The female mosquito is equipped with a proboscis, which she uses to pierce the human's skin and inject a little saliva before sucking the blood. Her saliva makes the blood more fluid, but it's also what makes you itch so much!

Three tricks an insect uses to detect its meals

✳ The horsefly detects its food with its 2 large, globular eyes. Each eye is made of over 3,000 simple eyes called ommatidia.

Ommatidia

✳ Bumblebees use their antennae to discover flower smells.

✳ Flies rub their feet together frequently to clean the tiny tufts of bristles they use to taste their food.

Bristles

Catch a tiny creature!

To get a close look at a tiny creature, catch it without injuring it.
And remember to let it go after you have observed it.

Use your hands

It isn't dangerous at all to carefully catch a snail, earthworm, slug, or beetle, either for you or for them.

Use a mouth aspirator

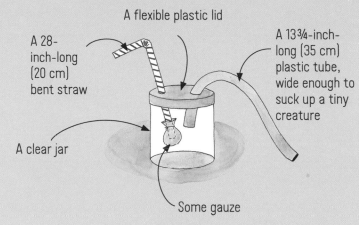

A flexible plastic lid

A 28-inch-long (20 cm) bent straw

A 13¾-inch-long (35 cm) plastic tube, wide enough to suck up a tiny creature

A clear jar

Some gauze

1. Punch 2 holes in the lid.

2. Use clear glue to position the straw in one hole and the tube in the other.

3. Use a rubber band to cover the end of the straw with a piece of gauze, so you don't suck a creature into your mouth!

Use a paintbrush

The tinier the creatures are, the more fragile they are. To catch one, gently use a flexible paintbrush to push it into a jar.

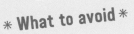

✳ What to avoid ✳

• Don't catch tiny creatures such as wasps, honeybees, or bumblebees that could sting you with their stinger.

• Also avoid butterflies and dragonflies—you could break their wings.

Your aspirator is ready! Gently suck on the straw to catch the tiny creature in the tube.

IN CASE OF ATTACK

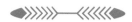

Flying is a very effective way to escape a predator, but it isn't always enough...

Blend in with vegetation

Some insects, and sometimes even their young, rely on their appearance to avoid the attention of their predators. They look like leaves, stems, or thin branches, especially when they don't move.

The peppered moth is nocturnal and perches on the trunk of a tree, flattening its wings against the bark to keep from being noticed during the day.

Display color

Other insects have elytrons (protective front wings) in bright colors, warning that they may be toxic or taste bad. Once a predator has gotten a taste of it, it won't try again the next time it sees one!

The Mylabris variabilis contains a substance that is irritating to any animal trying to eat it.

To scare away their predators, certain butterflies open their wings suddenly, displaying a vividly colored underside.

Peacock butterfly

The images that look like large eyes are called ocelli.

The Asian hornet uses its stinger to inject venom into its enemy's body.

Stinger

The bombardier beetle noisily shoots a burning, irritating substance at its assailant.

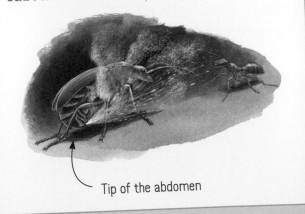

Tip of the abdomen

MIDAIR HUNTING

Tiny creatures hunt...

In-flight pursuit

The dragonfly manages to catch smaller insects, such as horseflies, while in flight.

Surprise

The crab spider perches on a flower and takes on its color. When an insect comes along, it pounces and injects its venom.

A brutal capture

Unmoving on the grass, a praying mantis suddenly thrusts its spine-covered forefeet (which fold like a Swiss Army knife) on its prey.

...or find themselves hunted!

Hunting on sight

Swallows fly with their beaks half open to catch little insects.

Catching in their wings

Bats hunt moths, knocking them toward their mouth with the membranes they use as wings.

Plucking with the beak

Titmice capture caterpillars in midair to feed to their young. They can catch 500 a day.

Two tiny creatures wait for their prey without moving. Which ones?

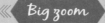
»»» Pollinators at work «««

Flying from flower to flower, pollinator insects allow plants produce fruit and seeds.

What are pollinators?

✳ Insects that carry flower pollen on their bodies, such as butterflies, flies, rose chafers, and, especially, many bees.

Rose chafer

Peacock butterfly

Fly

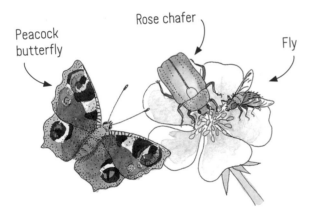

✳ There are 2,000 known species of bees in Europe, all of which carry pollen. Only one kind, the honeybee, lives in a beehive and makes honey.

What is pollination?

✳ When an insect leaves a flower after seeking the nectar (a sweet liquid) in its center, it carries away pollen grains.

Red mason bees also gather pollen to feed their larvae.

✳ When the insect reaches another flower, it drops some of the pollen grains. If the flower is the same species as the previous flower, it will become fruit.

How do honeybees live?

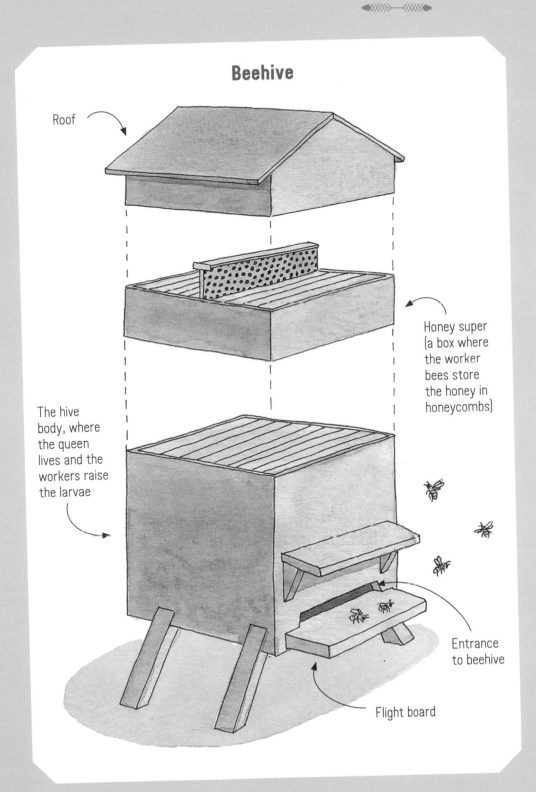

Beehive

Roof

Honey super (a box where the worker bees store the honey in honeycombs)

The hive body, where the queen lives and the workers raise the larvae

Entrance to beehive

Flight board

Who lives in a beehive?

1 queen, the mother of all the bees in the beehive

She lives 3 to 4 years.

3,000 males waiting to come out and reproduce

They live 21 days.

40,000 to 50,000 workers, who do all the work

They live 5 to 6 weeks.

Thousands of larvae, who become workers in 20 days

In the summer, as many as 2,000 are born every day.

The life of a worker bee

Once it becomes an adult, a worker spends almost its entire life in the beehive. Its tasks change as it gets older. At first, it cleans the cells; then it feeds the larvae, produces wax, and aerates the hive. It is only at the end of its life that it gets to gather nectar in the sun.

In the meadow

Common blue butterfly

Migrant hawker dragonfly

Caterpillar of the peacock butterfly

Cabbage moth

Bumblebee

Garden tiger-moth caterpillar

Marsh crane fly

Hoverfly

My observatory

1. Which butterfly uncoils its proboscis into a flower?

2. What hides an intense color on the underside of its wings?

3. What has very long hind legs?

4. What looks like a spider but hunts without a web?

Rose chafer

Hoverfly

Daddy longlegs, also called a crane fly or harvestman

Sawfly larva

Great green bush cricket

5. What has a very straight proboscis and 2 wings?

6. What looks like a mosquito but doesn't bite?

7. What kind of caterpillar is very hairy?

8. Which insect is often mistaken for a wasp?

CLOSE TO THE GROUND

WALKING, CRAWLING

The tiny creatures that live near the ground get around on their feet or crawl.

How many feet?

Arthropods are the only tiny creatures that have articulated legs.

* **Insects** always have 6 legs. They lift them up 3 at a time (2 on one side and 1 on the other, alternating).

* **Arachnids** move on 8 legs. Each leg consists of 7 jointed segments.

* **Myriapods** have more than 18 pairs of legs. To pull themselves forward, they raise them pair by pair, one after the other.

No legs!

* **Annelids:** Earthworms move forward by stretching and contracting their bodies, using the little bristles located on each of their rings to cling to their surroundings.

* **Mollusks:** Snails and slugs use the sticky slime (mucus) on their wide, muscular foot to move forward.

The leopard slug can extend itself up to 8 inches (20 cm).

Legs for leaping

A zebra back spider often gets around by small leaps. It propels itself by suddenly unbending its feet.

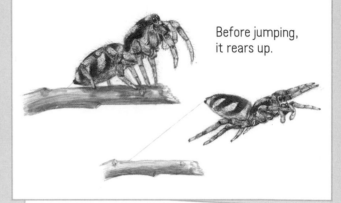

Before jumping, it rears up.

Legs for digging

The European mole cricket digs tunnels in the ground with its forefeet, which—like a mole's—look like shovels.

Legs for jumping and also for singing

The male locust produces its song by rubbing its hind legs, which have small teeth, against the thickened edges of its wings.

Build a snail terrarium!

A mosquito-netting type of screen cover for the snails to breathe without escaping

A damp sponge

Dirt from your garden or compost

An aquarium

※ Put your terrarium in your garden or on your balcony, protected from the sun and rain.

※ Head out and look for some snails after a good summer rain—that is when they are most active. Collect several if you want them to make babies, but don't put more than 4 or 5 in your terrarium.

※ Spray a little water every day on the dirt and on the sponge to keep the air humid. Add some fresh food: lettuce leaves or little pieces of carrot, radish, or mushroom. Also add some little bits of eggshell to provide the snails with the calcium they need to build their shells.

※ Watch your tiny, peaceable companions to see how they live…and if you want to release them, put them back in the place you caught them.

✳ Important ✳

Remove and replace food before it goes bad.

WHAT FEASTS!

The soil is a giant supermarket for tiny creatures. They all can find the food they like, on top or deep down.

Vegetarian menu

Many tiny creatures are herbivores. Crickets nibble on plants near the ground. Grasshopper or cicada larvae suck the sap from tree roots. Snails and slugs scrape green leaves with tongues covered with small teeth.

Steak for tiny creatures

Carnivorous tiny creatures consume other tiny animals. Spiders and millipedes feed, in particular, on insects. Earwigs eat aphids and caterpillars, along with a few flower petals.

The golden ground beetle runs after its prey and catches its weight in insects, worms, and slugs every night.

Small cleaners

Many tiny creatures feed on what they find on the ground: droppings, plants, and dead animals. They are called scavengers. Scavengers are indispensable for keeping nature healthy. By digesting waste, they clean it up and create fertile compost for plants.

Scavengers

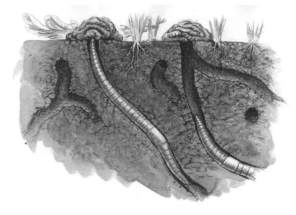

＊ Earthworms swallow dirt while digging vertical tunnels. They digest the remains of animals and plants.

＊ This tiny moss mite feeds on the droppings left by wood lice that have digested dead leaves.

＊ Burying beetles eat, among other things, the bodies of dead animals.

Meals for large animals

To nourish themselves, some large animals rely on tiny ground creatures.

Common toad

It sticks out its sticky tongue
to catch living prey.

European mole

It pursues earthworms underground
and bites them to paralyze them.

European hedgehog

It catches slugs, insects, and
sometimes earthworms.

The thrush, a musician

It eats a snail after breaking
its shell on a rock.

What stores its prey
underground?

CUNNING AND COMBAT

What kinds of attack tricks are used by the tiny creatures who live in the soil?

A poison weapon

Under a carpet of dead leaves, many tiny creatures use their venom to kill their prey. Scorpions sting; pseudoscorpions use two big claws instead of a stinger to inject their venom.

Pseudoscorpions attack small prey such as mites.

A murderous bite

Some spiders hunt on the ground: they spread layers of webbing or chase after their prey. When they bite their prey, their saliva softens its flesh.

A fatal trap

Adult ant lions look like dragonflies, but their larvae don't have wings and live in the ground. To trap their prey, they dig a funnel-shaped hole in fine sand, into which small insects such as ants fall.

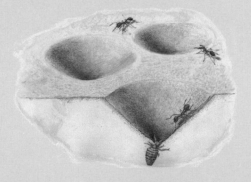

Ant lion larvae lie in wait for their prey in the bottom of their funnel.

How do tiny creatures defend themselves in the soil?

✳ The bloody-nosed beetle is an insect that can't fly or run fast. When it is attacked, it plays dead and shoots a toxic red liquid with its feet and head (but it isn't blood).

✳ The tiger beetle is an agile insect, but its larva has a soft abdomen that it hides in a vertical hole in the ground. To protect itself from attacks by its predators, it wears a kind of shield on its head.

✳ The common pill millipede, or pill bug, is a slow-moving myriapod. When it is disturbed, it rolls itself into a ball like a hedgehog, and its armored plates protect it.

Set up shelters in your garden!

To protect tiny creatures, create some
shelters where they can be safe.

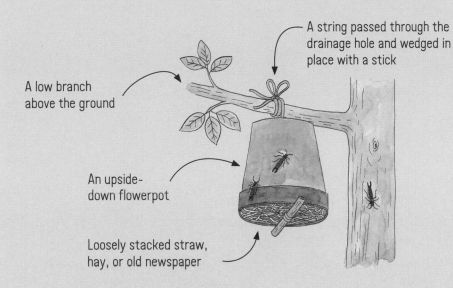

A string passed through the
drainage hole and wedged in
place with a stick

A low branch
above the ground

An upside-
down flowerpot

Loosely stacked straw,
hay, or old newspaper

Earwig hotel

In the daytime, earwigs will take
shelter in the flowerpot. When
night falls, they will come out
and attack aphids.

Inns for tiny creatures

In a corner of your yard, make a pile
of branches or big pebbles on the
ground; they will provide lots
of hiding places for snails and wood
lice, who don't like dryness or light.
You can watch them by lifting
up a branch or a rock.

A pile of dead leaves
can serve as a pantry
for springtails, earthworms,
and insects such as rove
beetles, who are mostly
active at night.

>>>>> Ant society <<<<<

Ants live in colonies. Together, they build their nest, the anthill, for raising their larvae. Let's go find some wood ants.

Who lives in an anthill?

✳ The males and young females: they have wings and wait to reproduce during their one and only mating flight. There are about ten males for every hundred females.

✳ The queens: Wood ants have several of them. These are big females who have lost their wings after being inseminated. They lay dozens of eggs a day.

✳ The workers: These are little wingless females who don't reproduce. There are a great many of them. They tend the larvae and supply and defend the anthill.

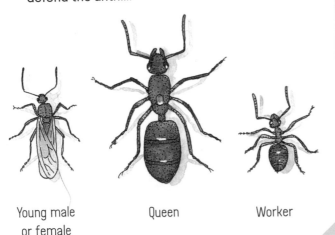

Young male   Queen   Worker
or female

How do wood ants find food?

When an exploring worker finds something to eat, it comes back to the anthill, leaving an odor behind it. Then all the others need to do is follow the trail. Wood ants capture tiny creatures, especially caterpillars.

How do ants recognize each other?

They regularly clean their own and each others' bodies and antennae, which mixes their odors, creating a one-of-a-kind scent shared by the whole colony.

A guided tour of an anthill

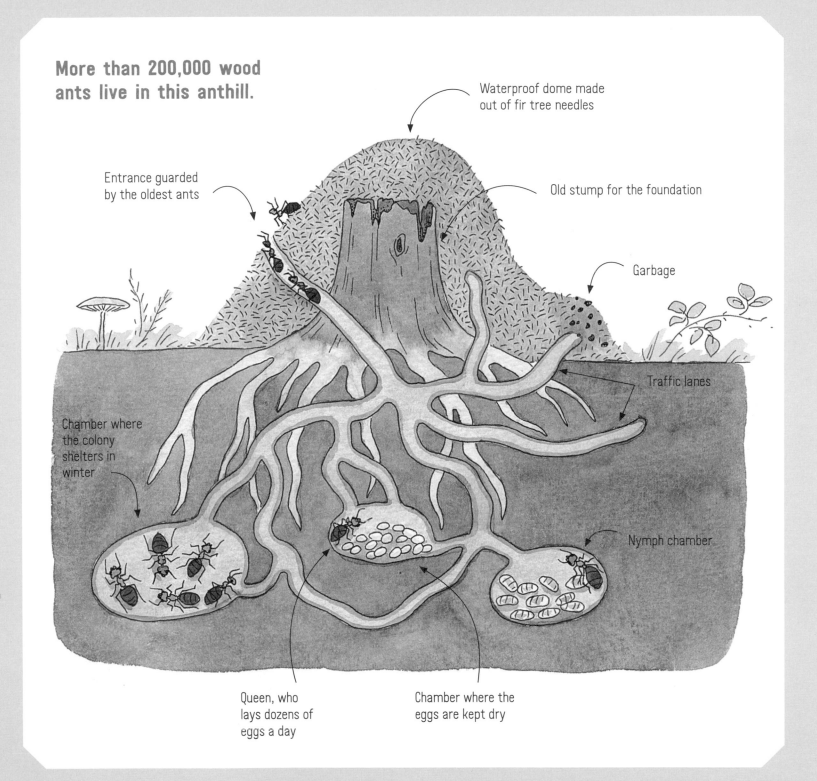

More than 200,000 wood ants live in this anthill.

Waterproof dome made out of fir tree needles

Old stump for the foundation

Entrance guarded by the oldest ants

Garbage

Traffic lanes

Chamber where the colony shelters in winter

Nymph chamber

Queen, who lays dozens of eggs a day

Chamber where the eggs are kept dry

In the forest

Spider wasp

Earwig

Brown hive snail

Two-colored mason bee

Red wiggler worms

Wood lice

My observatory

1. What raises its larvae in a little burrow?

2. What has more than 40 pairs of little legs?

3. What is munching on a mushroom?

4. What is attacking the spider?

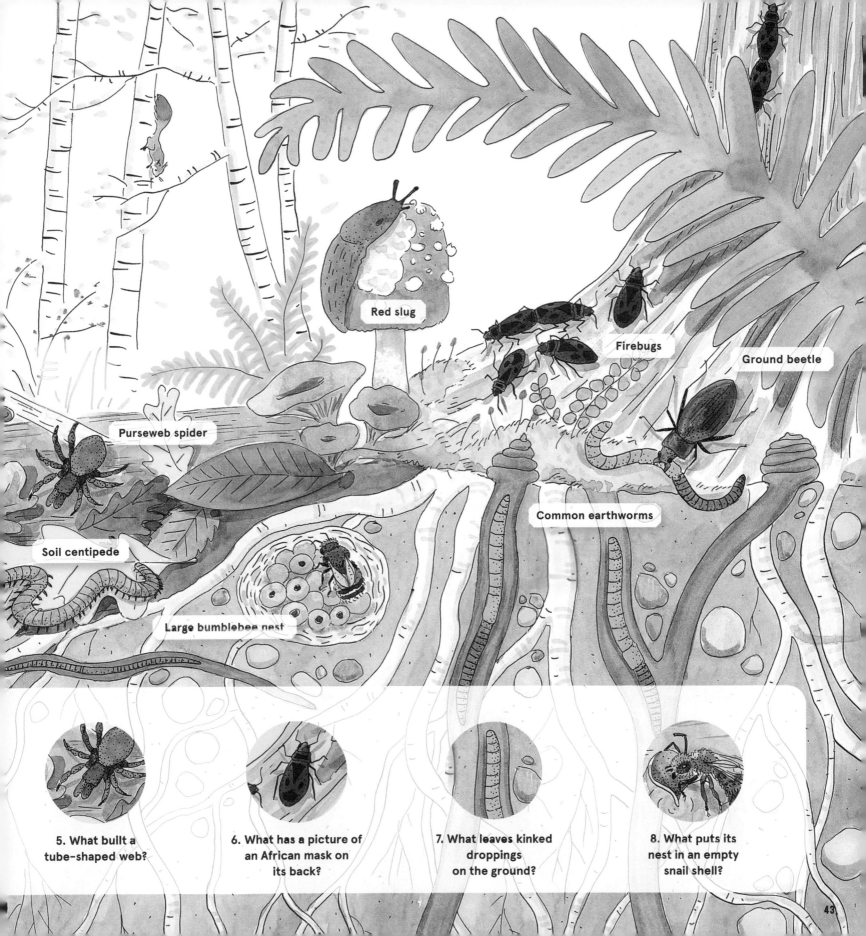

Red slug

Firebugs

Ground beetle

Purseweb spider

Common earthworms

Soil centipede

Large bumblebee nest

5. What built a tube-shaped web?

6. What has a picture of an African mask on its back?

7. What leaves kinked droppings on the ground?

8. What puts its nest in an empty snail shell?

IN THE WATER

SWIMMING

Many tiny creatures live in streams and ponds. How do they get around?

Rowing

Aquatic insects that live in the open water get around by swimming. They wave their long hind legs—which are flattened and equipped with a fringe of bristles—like a pair of oars. Some, such as water boatmen and predaceous diving beetles, swim on their abdomens. Some, such as backswimmers, swim on their backs.

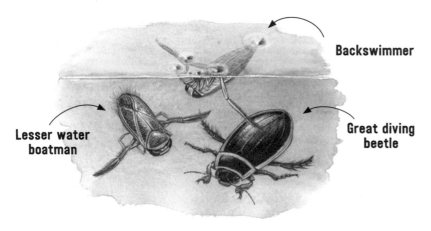

Backswimmer

Lesser water boatman

Great diving beetle

Scuttling

Some tiny creatures, like freshwater shrimp, get around by swimming or walking on the bottom of a body of water. While aquatic-insect larvae can't swim very well, they propel themselves by grabbing submerged plants.

Crawling

Mollusks move around on their single foot. The pond snail uses its sticky mucus to crawl upside down under the surface of the water. Ramshorns glide on water plants. Freshwater mussels move on the bottom by stretching out their foot or shooting water from their shell.

Gliding on the surface

Water striders skate on the water.

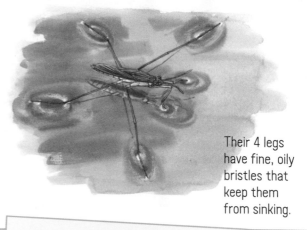

Their 4 legs have fine, oily bristles that keep them from sinking.

Raft spiders walk and run on the surface of marshes.

Sometimes they use their hind legs to grab floating plants and hide in the water.

Whirligig beetles float on the surface and use their short hind legs to paddle jerkily.

They dive or start whirling when disturbed.

Hind leg covered with bristles

Above the water

Damselflies

These insects flit around lightly. Their front and rear wings have the same shape. At rest, the wings are joined together or scarcely open.

Male small red damselfly

Male banded demoiselle

Male emerald damselfly

Dragonflies

Dragonflies are powerful fliers. Their back wings have a wider base than their front ones. Their wings remain spread open when fully at rest.

Male western clubtail

Male scarlet dragonfly

Male broad-bodied chaser

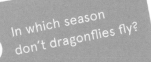

In which season don't dragonflies fly?

BREATHING IN THE WATER

Tiny aquatic creatures all need oxygen, but they don't all breathe the same way.

With lungs

Some tiny creatures, like water snails, have lungs. They regularly rise to the water's surface to breathe, then their hemolymph distributes oxygen from the air throughout their bodies (unlike insects).

With gills

Other tiny aquatic creatures have gills to extract the oxygen dissolved in water and send it to their hemolymph. They need to replenish the water that comes into contact with their gills regularly. To do this, freshwater mussels open their shells, while crustaceans wave their legs constantly.

Water lice create a flow of water toward their gills by flapping their legs.

Bottom view

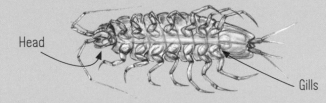

Head

Gills

With tracheae

Insects and arachnids have tracheae instead of gills or lungs. These are small, very narrow, tubes where air circulates, distributing the oxygen in the air directly to various parts of their bodies.

Diving with spare air

Tiny water creatures keep their tracheae supplied by taking in air at the surface.

Siphon

✳ Water stick insects take air in through a siphon and store it under their wings, at the opening to their tracheae.

✳ Diving bell spiders create an underwater reservoir for themselves: they weave a web between plants and fill it with air bubbles gathered from the surface.

✳ Great silver water beetles stick their heads out of the water and, using their antennae, channel air bubbles to their thorax and abdomen, where they trap them in their fine bristles.

Thorax   Abdomen

How aquatic larvae breathe

With gills

Mayfly larvae have gills all along their abdomens to breathe and to stabilize them when swimming.

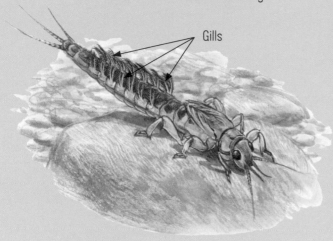

Gills

With tracheae and gills

Dragonfly larvae supply their tracheae with oxygen using gills located in a pocket at the tip of their abdomens.

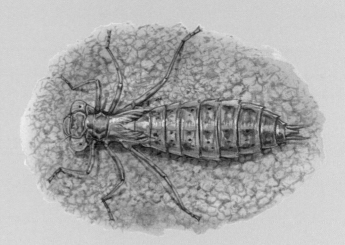

Caddis fly larvae have gills, but they are hidden by a sheath of grains of sand or twigs that protects their soft abdomens. They have to undulate this sheath constantly to keep fresh water touching their gills.

Through the skin

Midge larvae do not have gills, and their tracheae don't yet function. They absorb oxygen from the water through their skin.

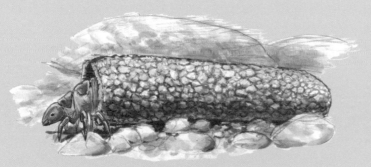

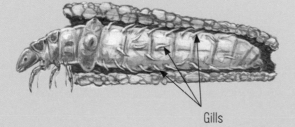

Gills

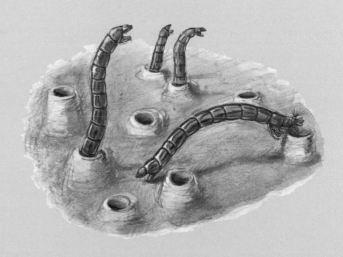

EATING, CLEANING

When tiny aquatic creatures eat, it helps to clean the water.

Water filters

Some tiny creatures, such as bivalves, guzzle a lot of water and then eject it, keeping only the microorganisms and animal/plant waste on which they feed. In other words, they filter water by removing small debris from it.

The water enters through a siphon and and comes out filtered from the other end.

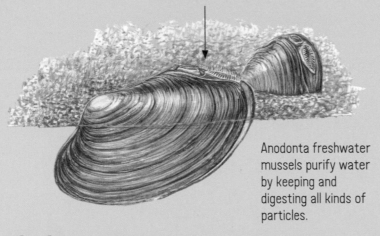

Anodonta freshwater mussels purify water by keeping and digesting all kinds of particles.

Surface sweepers

Water striders, whirligig beetles, and water measurers are insects that use their legs to detect vibrations created on the surface by little animals that are drowning. They glide across the water to catch them before they fall to the bottom.

Bottom scrubbers

Dead animals and plants build up on the bottom of ponds and lakes. Water lice and caddis fly larvae clean the muck by eating them.

Hunting in the depths

✳ Water scorpions crouch on the bottom of ponds and pounce on any prey passing by, catching it between their sharp forelegs. They can fly away and change ponds if they don't have enough water or food.

✳ As soon as they spot prey, dragonfly larvae propel themselves by shooting out water they store in the back of their abdomen. Next, they stick out a kind of hinged pincer called a mask.

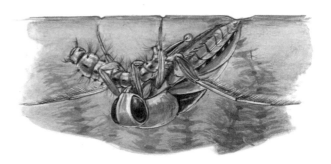

✳ A backswimmer hunts its prey (worms, insects, little fish) while swimming. When it catches the prey, it injects digestive juices into it, liquefying its organs to suck them up.

Four ways to eat

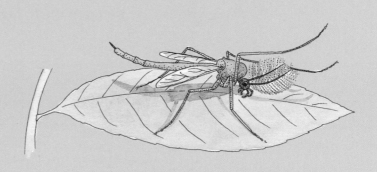

1. How do water stick insects hunt their prey?

- A They hunt it while swimming.
- B They catch it by surprise.
- C They lure it into a trap.

2. The larvae of midges feed in the mud. But what do adult winged midges eat?

- A They gather flower nectar.
- B They suck blood.
- C They don't eat.

3. Who hunts freshwater shrimp?

- A Water striders
- B Dragonfly larvae
- C Other shrimp

4. How do great diving beetles kill their prey in open water?

- A They bite it.
- B They sting it.
- C They drown it.

Life in the water

**Many tiny creatures are born in pond or lake water.
Some spend their whole lives there, while others don't.**

Life cycle of the culex mosquito

Culex mosquitoes spend the first 3 weeks of their
life in the water before taking flight for 2 to 3 weeks.

1. Eggs

Laid on the surface of stagnant water in groups of 30 to 200, they float like mini rafts.

4. Nymphs

They don't eat and remain at the surface to breathe. They undergo huge transformations: their legs and wings appear.

2. Larvae

Two days after spawning, they come out of the egg underwater. They feed by filtering water and rise to the surface to take in air.

5. Metamorphosis

At the end of 2 to 5 days, the shell surrounding the nymph splits and the adult culex mosquito climbs out of the water. As soon as its wings are stiff, it flies away.

3. Molting

Larvae molt: They change their skin 3 times while growing. By the time they are 20 days old, they are .4 inch (1 cm) long. They molt one more time and then become nymphs.

6. Adult

Once they are adults, the males and females mate. Only females bite because they need to eat blood to nourish their eggs. The males gather flower nectar.

Life cycle of the great diving beetle

Great diving beetles are insects that are born, grow, and spend almost their whole life in the water.

1. Eggs

The females dig into the stem of an underwater plant to lay their eggs.

4. Nymphs

The larvae transform into nymphs and come out of the water. They dig a shelter on shore, where they become immobile. They are preparing to take their new adult form.

2. Larvae

At the beginning of summer, the larvae leave their egg. They come to the surface to breathe, with their heads upside down, and eat a whole lot!

5. Metamorphosis

Two weeks later, the predaceous diving beetle transforms into an adult. It measures about 1.2 inches (3 cm) long. It leaves its shelter or stays there until the following spring.

3. Molting

The larvae molt 3 times in 5 to 6 weeks. They grow to 2 to 2.4 inches (5 to 6 cm). They feed on small fish, tadpoles, or other larvae.

6. Adult

It flies away from the shore to find the ideal pond and reproduce. When it is in the water, it hangs upside down near the surface to breathe: it stores a supply of air under its wings. It can live 2 to 3 years.

At the seashore

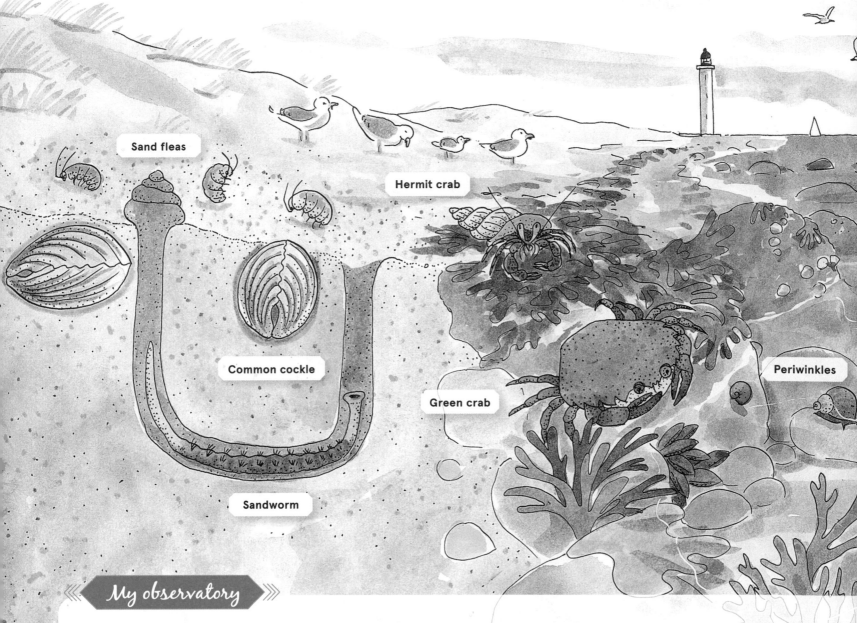

Sand fleas

Hermit crab

Common cockle

Green crab

Periwinkles

Sandworm

My observatory

1. What shelters from the sun and birds in a puddle of water?

2. What has crab claws and hides in a shell?

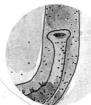

3. What leaves coiled castings on the beach?

4. What looks for moisture but does not live in water?

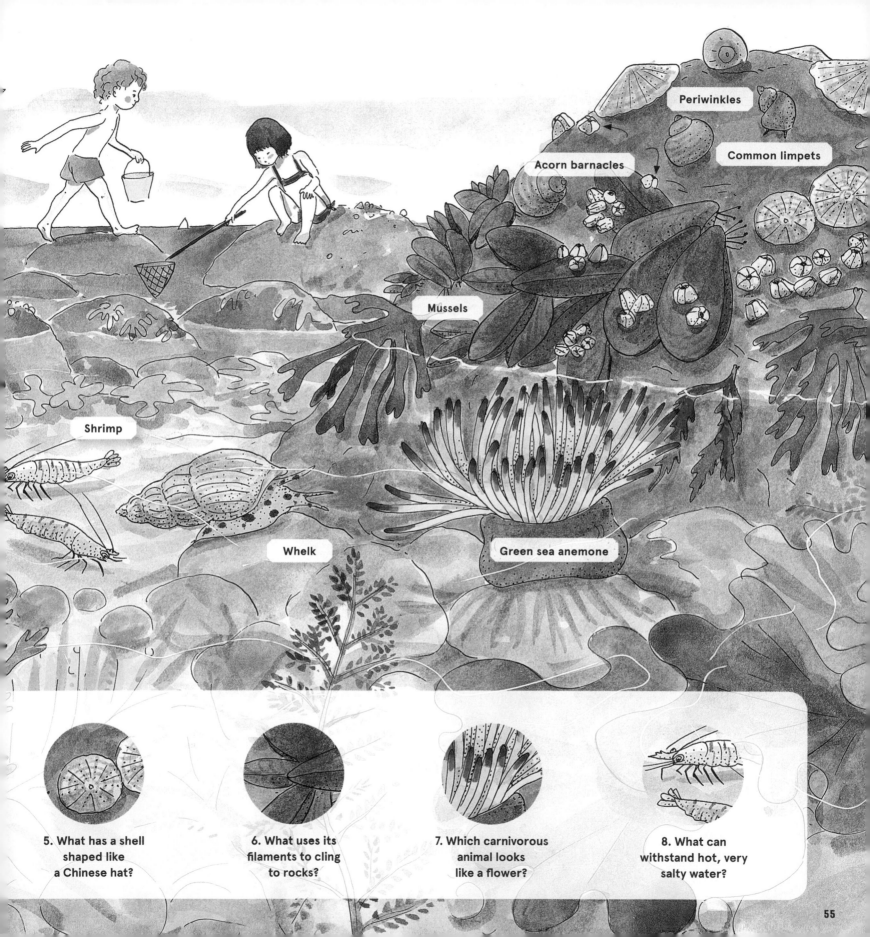

Periwinkles

Common limpets

Acorn barnacles

Mussels

Shrimp

Whelk

Green sea anemone

5. What has a shell shaped like a Chinese hat?

6. What uses its filaments to cling to rocks?

7. Which carnivorous animal looks like a flower?

8. What can withstand hot, very salty water?

INCREDIBLE CREATURES

World records

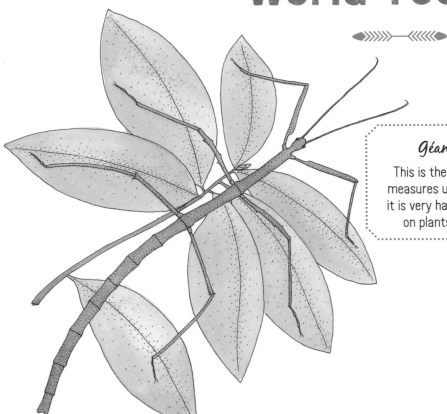

Géant Indonesian leaf insect

This is the world's biggest insect! The female measures up to 20 inches (50 cm) in length. But it is very hard to spot because it holds very still on plants. It lives on the island of Borneo.

Rhinoceros beetle

It can measure up to 6 inches (15 cm) in length. The male uses its horn to lift its rival and toss it on the ground. It is one of the strongest insects in Europe.

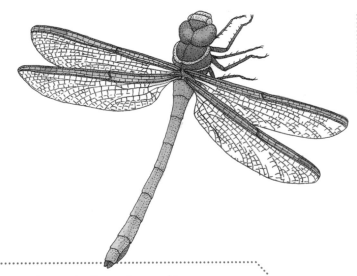

Giant Australian dragonfly

It can fly over 35 miles per hour (55 km/h) and can reach a speed of 45 miles per hour (70 km/h) when borne on the wind, making it the world's fastest insect.

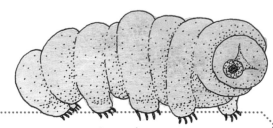

Tardigrade

It's less than a 10th of an inch long (1 mm), but it's the toughest of all invertebrate animals: it can come back to life after being frozen and can withstand a trip in space.

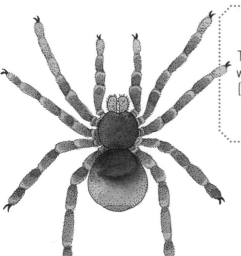

Goliath birdeater

This is the biggest spider in the world. It has a span of 11 inches (28 cm) and weighs 4 ¼ ounces (120 g). Its abdomen is as big as a fist. It lives in Guyana.

Attacus atlas moth

This moth's wings can be as long as 10 to 12 inches (25 to 30 cm), the same span as a sparrow's. It lives in Southeast Asia.

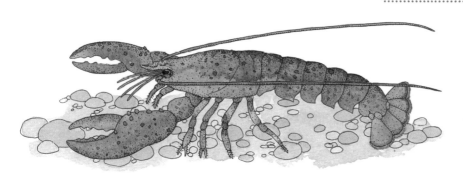

Lobster

One lobster that was raised in an aquarium was around 140 years old when it was set free in the sea (in an area where fishing is prohibited), making it the oldest arthropod on record.

Little Barrier Island giant weta

The heaviest insect on Earth! Right before a female lays her eggs, she can weigh around 2½ ounces (70 g), the same as 3 mice would weigh together, and is 4 inches (10 cm) long! It lives in New Zealand.

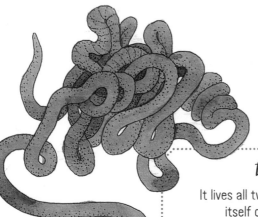

Bootlace worm

It lives all twisted up, but if it stretched itself out, it would be 100 feet (30 m) long, as long as 3 buses! It is found in the North Sea.

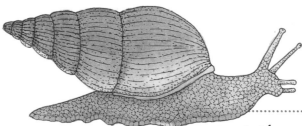

Giant African snail

With a shell 4 inches (10 cm) in diameter, it's the world's biggest snail. It weighs almost 2¼ pounds (1 kg), including its shell, the same as what a dwarf rabbit weighs. It is a native of Africa.

The most beautiful butterflies

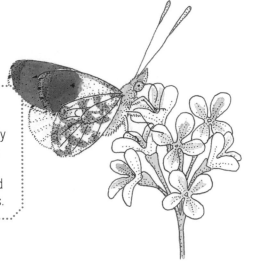

Orange tip

Only the male of this butterfly species has an orange spot on the tip of its wings. Before winter, adults die and caterpillars turn into nymphs.

Monarch butterfly

This butterfly spends summer in Canada and in the northern United States. It flies over 1,800 miles (3,000 km) to spend the winter in the forests of Mexico.

Queen Alexandra's birdwing

It lives in the forests of Papua New Guinea. It is one of the biggest butterflies. The female, which is larger than the male, can reach a width of 11 inches (28 cm).

Swallowtail butterfly

By day, it flies above the dry, hot prairies in bloom. The male patrols his territory to keep his rivals from intruding. It lives in Europe.

Luna moth

It flies in the forests of North America at night. The male's large antennae allow him to detect the odor given off by the females.

Five-spot burnet

It gathers nectar from the clover blooming in sunny, humid prairies. Its colors tell its predators that it has a bad taste and that they should avoid eating it!

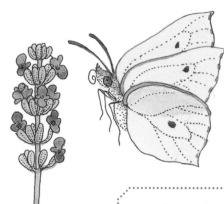

Brimstone butterfly

It's one of the first butterflies to take flight in our gardens during the spring, after spending winter in a hiding place. The male is bright yellow, while the female is paler.

Great peacock moth

It is one of Europe's biggest butterflies. It doesn't have a tongue and can't feed itself. It can fly for about a week using the reserves it stores up when it is a caterpillar.

Morpho

It lives in the tropical forests of South America. Its wings are covered with transparent scales that reflect a pretty blue light.

Oleander hawk moth

This butterfly, active at dusk, leaves Europe in the fall and flies to Africa, where it spends the winter. Its caterpillar feeds on young oleander leaves, which are toxic.

Pests

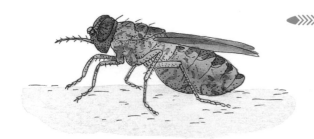

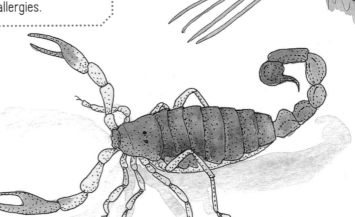

Tsetse fly

It lives only in Africa, south of the Sahara. It bites humans and livestock to feed on their blood. It can transmit sometimes fatal diseases, such as sleeping sickness.

Tick

It lives on plants and is attracted to warm bodies. It attaches tightly to the skin of a mammal and sucks its blood, sometimes transmitting diseases.

Pine processionary caterpillar

At the end of winter, the caterpillar leaves its silken nest nestled in pine trees and drops to the ground to metamorphose into a butterfly. Its bristles sometimes cause violent allergies.

Common wasp

Unlike bees, who die when they sting their victim, wasps can sting several times to defend themselves.

Tube web spider

It may bite your skin if you squeeze it, but its bite isn't dangerous.

Indian red scorpion

It lives in India and Pakistan. Its bite is dangerous, sometimes fatal, to humans because its paralytic venom is one of the strongest produced by any scorpion.

Chigger

The adult lays its eggs in meadows. The larvae, to feed themselves, inject their saliva under our skin, causing unpleasant itching.

Flea

The larvae live on the ground, and the adults can jump as high as 12 inches (30 cm) onto a dog, a cat, or a human. They bite and feed on blood.

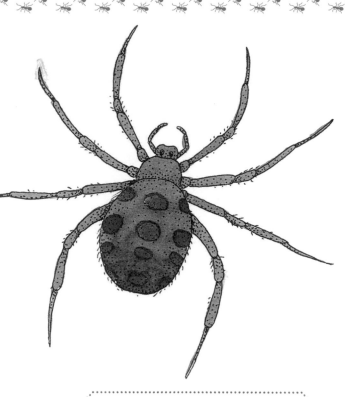

European black widow

This spider, found in both Corsica and on the European continent, kills its prey by biting it and injecting it with venomous saliva. It can be painful when it accidentally bites a human.

Louse

It clings to people's heads and uses its hooked feet to move around people's hair. It bites the scalp to suck a little blood. It doesn't transmit any diseases.

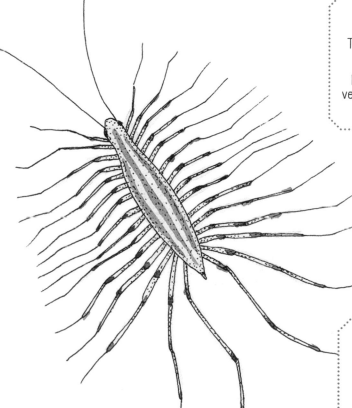

House centipede

It uses its venom to kill its prey but only bites people if grabbed by our fingers. Its bite hurts but isn't dangerous.

Nocturnal creatures

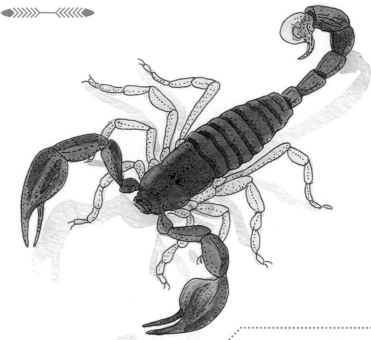

Great capricorn beetle

Its larva develops for 3 to 5 years and feeds on wood. The adult hides under the bark of a tree trunk all day long. It takes flight only at nightfall.

European yellow-tailed scorpion

It hides under a stone and hunts tiny creatures at night. Its sting isn't dangerous for humans. The female carries her young on her back for several weeks.

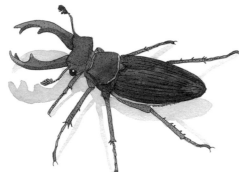

Stag beetle

To feed itself, the larva digs into the living tree. The adult licks tree sap. At nightfall, it buzzes around near groves of trees.

Leopard moth

The caterpillar feeds on fruit tree leaves. The adult lives just for a few days; it doesn't have a proboscis, so it can't eat anything. It spends its time against a tree trunk and flies away at dusk.

Red underwing butterfly

During the day, it doesn't move and sits on the bark of a tree with its wings folded.
If it is disturbed, it flies away, spreading its wings. Their red interior frightens predators.

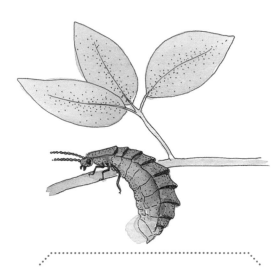

Brimstone moth

It doesn't move during the day. It never flies very far at night. Its caterpillar looks like a twig on a tree. The adult looks like a yellow leaf on a tree.

Glowworm

In spite of its name, it isn't a worm—it's an insect. The female doesn't have any wings. A greenish light at the end of her abdomen serves as a beacon for the male, who flies to her.

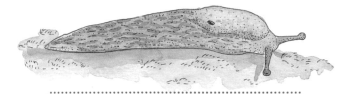

Banana slug

It moves around at night. It uses its 2 pairs of tentacles to detect light and odors. In case of danger, it retracts them.

Death's-head hawk moth

This extra-large butterfly gets its name from the spots on its thorax. During the day, it folds its wings like a tent on top of its body.

Wood louse spider

It spends its days sheltering in its silken lodge. It hunts wood lice at night, piercing their carapace with its strong hooks.

Guests in our homes

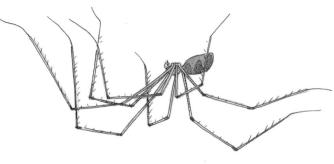

Longbodied cellar spider

It often lives in cellars and the nooks and crannies of rooms. It hangs upside down under its web. When disturbed, it makes its web vibrate until it becomes invisible.

Indian meal moth

This little butterfly lays eggs in flour or cereal. The caterpillars secrete silk threads that make food inedible.

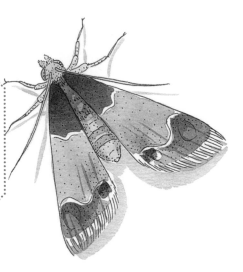

Silverfish

The "silver" part of its name is because its body is covered with tiny silver scales. It eats the flour and sugar it finds in houses and even nibbles on paper!

Cockroach

It is a native of tropical regions and can survive only in heated, humid buildings. The female protects her eggs in an ootheca.

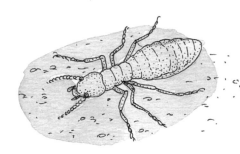

Eastern Mediterranean termite

It flees from light by inhabiting a building's framework and floors, where it does a great deal of damage by nibbling on the wood. These termites live in colonies the way ants do.

Common clothes moth

In nature, this moth and its larva feed on feathers and hairs. They have adapted to our homes, and their caterpillars make themselves at home in wool or silk clothes.

Daddy longlegs

It looks like a giant mosquito, but it doesn't bite. It is attracted by light and enters homes. They're also called crane flies.

Small tortoiseshell butterfly

The adult can live up to 10 months by wintering in an attic or barn. Its caterpillar grows on nettles in the spring.

Giant house spider

It weaves solid webs, then lurks in them to capture its prey. It doesn't bite humans.

House cricket

It seeks out the warmth of houses. It especially likes to hang out in bakeries and subways. The female lays her eggs in moist ground.

Housefly

It feeds only on liquids that it mops up with its proboscis from rotting refuse or our foods, where it lays its eggs.

The insect orchestra

Locusts
Males chirr (or stridulate) to seduce their sweetheart.

Grasshoppers
They stridulate by rubbing their short elytrons together.

Crickets
The males stridulate by scraping their right elytron on their left elytron.

Water boatman
The males stridulate by rubbing their ridged forelegs on the sides of their head.

Burying beetles
They stridulate by rubbing their elytrons against a rough section of their abdomens.

Cicadas
Males chirr by clicking together membranes in their abdomens.

Bombardier beetles
They produce an explosion by expelling liquid held in their abdomen.

Mosquitoes
They buzz by vibrating their wings.

Bumblebees
They hum by vibrating the walls of their thorax and pushing air through the opening of their tracheae.

Death's-head hawk moths
When disturbed, they expel air through their proboscis to squeak like a mouse.

ANSWERS TO QUESTIONS

Who are the tiny creatures?

P. 13, Quiz: 1c, 2a, 3b, 4c
PP. 18–19, My observatory:
1. Ladybug larva
2. Wood louse 3. Leaf-cutter bee
4. Adonis blue caterpillar
5. Black spruce weevil
6. Gray garden slug
7. Green shield bug
8. Garden snail

Life in the sky

P. 23: Swallowtail butterfly
P. 27: Crab spider and praying mantis
PP. 30–31, My observatory:
1. Cabbage moth 2. Common blue
butterfly 3. Great green bush cricket
4. Daddy longlegs 5. Greater bee fly
6. Marsh crane fly 7. Garden tiger-
moth caterpillar 8. Hoverfly

Close to the ground

P. 37: European mole
PP. 42–43, My observatory:
1. Earwig 2. Soil centipede
3. Red slug 4. Spider wasp
5. Purseweb spider
6. Firebug 7. Earthworm
8. Two-colored mason bee

In the water

P. 47: In winter
P. 51, Quiz: 1b, 2c, 3b, 4a
P. 54–55, My observatory:
1. Green crab 2. Hermit crab
3. Sandworm 4. Sand flea
5. Common limpet 6. Mussel
7. Green sea anemone
8. Shrimp

⋙ Index ⋘

A
Acorn barnacle 55
Adonis blue butterfly 18, 19
Anodonta freshwater mussel 50
Ant 18, 40–41
Ant lion 38
Aphid 12, 18
Asian hornet 26
Attacus atlas moth 59
Azure damselfly 13

B
Backswimmer 46, 50
Banana slug 65
Banded demoiselle 47
Beetle 22
Black spruce weevil 19
Bloody-nosed beetle 38
Bombardier beetle 26, 68
Bootlace worm 59
Brimstone butterfly 61
Brimstone moth 65
Broad-bodied chaser 47
Brown hive snail 42
Bumblebee 19, 24, 30, 43, 68
Burying beetle 36, 68

C
Cabbage moth 30
Caddis fly 40
Cellar slug 11
Cheese snail 15
Chigger 63
Cicada 16, 36, 68
Clam worm 11
Cockroach 66
Common blue butterfly 30
Common centipede 10
Common clothes moth 66
Common cockle 54
Common earthworm 43
Common limpet 55
Common pill millipede 38
Crab spider 27
Cricket 68
Culex mosquito 52

D
Daddy longlegs 31, 67
Damselfly 47
Death's-head hawk moth 65, 68
Diadem spider 15
Diving bell spider 48
Dragonfly 27, 49, 50
Dung beetle 13

E
Earthworm 11, 36
Earwig 36, 39, 42
Eastern Mediterranean termite 66
Emerald damselfly 47
European black widow 63
European hornet 23
European mole cricket 34
European yellow-tailed scorpion 64

F
Field cricket 12
Firebug 43
Fish bloodsucker 11
Five-spot burnet 61
Flat periwinkle 11
Flea 63
Fly 22, 24, 28
Four-spotted skimmer 22
Freshwater shrimp 10, 51

G
Gall wasp 13
Garden banded snail 35
Garden snail 11, 18
Garden tiger moth 12, 30
Giant African snail 59
Giant Australian dragonfly 58
Giant house spider 67
Giant Indonesian leaf insect 58
Glowworm 65
Goliath birdeater 59
Grasshopper 24, 36, 68
Gray garden slug 18
Great capricorn beetle 64
Great diving beetle 46, 51, 53
Great green bush cricket 31
Great peacock moth 61
Great silver water beetle 48
Green crab 54
Green lacewing 23
Green sea anemone 55
Green shield bug 18
Ground beetle 36, 43
Grove snail 11

H
Hazelnut weevil 13
Hermit crab 54
Honeybee 14, 28, 29
Horsefly 24
House centipede 63
House cricket 67
Housefly 67
Hoverfly 19, 30, 31
Hummingbird hawk moth 24

I
Indian meal moth 66
Indian red scorpion 62

J
Julid 16

L
Ladybug 18
Leaf-cutter bee 19
Leopard moth 64
Leopard slug 34
Lesser water boatman 46
Little Barrier Island giant weta 59
Lobster 59
Locust 22, 34, 68
Longbodied cellar spider 66
Louse 63
Luna moth 60

M
Marsh crane fly 30
Mayfly 23, 49
Midge 49, 51
Migrant hawker dragonfly 30
Monarch butterfly 60
Morpho 61
Mosquito 24, 68
Moss mite 36
Mussel 55
Mylabris variabilis 26

O
Old-world swallowtail 23
Oleander hawk moth 61
Orange tip 60
Orb weaver spider 10, 19

P
Painted lady butterfly 17
Parent bug 14
Peacock butterfly 26, 28, 30
Peppered moth 26
Periwinkle 54, 55
Pine processionary caterpillar 62
Pond snail 11
Praying mantis 12, 27
Pseudoscorpion 38
Purseweb spider 43

Q
Queen Alexandra's birdwing 60

R
Raft spider 46
Red cabbage bug 23
Red mason bee 28
Red slug 43
Red underwing butterfly 65
Red wiggler worm 42
Rhinoceros beetle 58
Rose chafer 14, 28, 31
Rove beetle 39
Rustic limpet 11

S
Sand flea 54
Sandworm 54
Sawfly 31
Scarlet dragonfly 47
Seven-spot ladybug 15, 19
Shrimp 55
Silverfish 66
Small red damselfly 47
Small tortoiseshell butterfly 67
Snail 12, 35
Soil centipede 43
Spider wasp 42
Stag beetle 64
Swallowtail butterfly 23, 60

T
Tarantula wolf spider 12
Tardigrade 58
Tick 62
Tiger beetle 38
Tsetse fly 62
Tube web spider 62
Two-colored mason bee 42

W
Wasp 10, 62
Wasp spider 12
Water boatman 68
Water louse 48
Water scorpion 50
Water stick insect 48, 51
Water strider 46
Western clubtail 47
Whelk 55
Whirligig beetle 46
White plume moth 23
Wolf spider 14
Wood ant 40, 41
Wood louse 18, 39, 42
Wood louse spider 65

Z
Zebra back spider 34

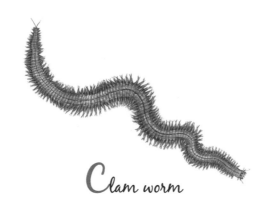

Clam worm

Red mason bee

Rustic limpet

Tarantula wolf spider

Water stick insect

Grasshopper

Crab spider